HIGH PRAISE FOR *SPEECHLESS*

Speechless has gained praise from the disability community for its realistic portrayal of disability. The family's life does not completely revolve around J.J. and his cerebral palsy. It is part of the show, but they are very much a normal family. In fact, sometimes, J.J. is portrayed as a bit of a jerk! This is a portrayal of disabled people that many shows and movies have shied away from, but it is a real part of disability—like everyone, disabled people can be rude sometimes!

Just a Regular Family

In the past, representations of disability have sometimes made the person with a disability look like a perfect person who never experiences real feelings like anger or sadness. In *Speechless*, J.J. is very much a typical brother to his siblings in that he can be grouchy, funny, sad, or a practical joker. His siblings treat him like an ordinary brother, too, just as most real-life siblings of people with disabilities do.

Normalizing Disability

If the entertainment industry continues to put forth efforts like *Speechless*, where disabled people are included in the process and accurately represented, it will continue to break the stigma of disability and normalize it for the viewing public. And it will create more opportunities for actors like Micah Fowler, who previously had little opportunity. Interestingly, though J.J. on *Speechless* cannot speak, Micah Fowler can. He speaks with difficulty, but he can speak, and he does in his everyday life. Sometimes, he has said, it is difficult for him not to speak when he's in character. He is not used to having to compensate for a lack of ability to speak with exaggerated gestures and facial expressions.

Fowler has also assumed the role of ambassador for the Cerebral Palsy Foundation. An avid fan of television and film since he was a child, Fowler was disappointed to not see many characters with disabilities in movies or in television shows. He hopes to one day appear in a *Star Wars* or a Marvel film.

Glee, a popular television series that ran from 2009 to 2015, featured a character with Down syndrome who was played by an actress with the condition. The show was praised for its realistic portrayal of a teen with Down syndrome. Reality television does not always shy away from featuring people with disabilities, either. There have been several shows featuring families with dwarfism, and the Emmy Award–winning *Born This Way* follows the lives of seven young adults with Down syndrome. Shows like these help break the stereotypes that have been reinforced by the entertainment field in the past.

Promoting Diversity in Entertainment

Entertainment is meant to amuse and interest audiences but it also has another effect: What is portrayed in entertainment can be normalized for the general public. For example, people of different races, cultures, and abilities were once seen as something to be feared or avoided. Seeing these different groups of people represented in the entertainment field helps audiences understand more about them and appreciate them.

Lauren Potter, who was diagnosed with Down syndrome at birth, portrayed cheerleader Becky Jackson in *Glee*.

CRITICAL
THINKING
QUESTION:
James Durbin, a fourth-place finisher on *American Idol* and the lead singer of Quiet Riot, has Asperger's syndrome, a type of autism. How do you think different abilities might affect musicians and others in the field?

It can work the other way, too, though. If stereotypes are reinforced by the industry, it can cement those stereotypes in people's minds. Diversity in entertainment can help break down negative stereotypes and reinforce accurate depictions of various groups of people. But diversity in entertainment has another benefit, too. It shows young audiences what is possible. Young black girls interested in a career in music need look no further than Beyoncé to see that it is possible. Asian children in the United States who dream of a career as an actor or screenwriter can look at Academy Award nominee Kumail Nanjiani as an example of what can be. Girls who want to be strong women can look at musicians and actresses like Pink, Emma Watson, and Lupita Nyong'o.

Hopefully, the entertainment industry will continue its upward trend of featuring and employing more diverse people in the areas of race, gender, culture, ability, and economic background to accurately represent the great diversity that makes up the population of the United States.

Singer Beyoncé is an inspiration to many but especially to young black girls. Here she is performing on the *Today Show* in 2006.

Timeline

1911: *An Indian Love Story* becomes the first film to use Native American actors in its cast.

1928: Silent-film star Gloria Swanson forms a production company to produce her own film.

1939: Hattie McDaniel is the first black woman to win an Academy Award, winning for *Gone with the Wind*.

1948: José Ferrer becomes the first Latinx actor to be nominated for an Academy Award. Ferrer lost in 1948 but won Best Actor in 1950.

1950: Ethel Waters becomes the first black woman to be featured on a sitcom.

1958: Sidney Poitier becomes the first black man to be nominated for an Academy Award, for *The Defiant Ones*.

1958: Diahann Carroll becomes the first black actor or actress to be nominated for an Emmy Award.

1958: Count Basie becomes the first black man to win a Grammy Award.

1958: Ella Fitzgerald becomes the first black woman to win a Grammy Award.

1961: Rita Moreno becomes the first Latinx to win an Academy Award for Best Supporting Actress.

1963: Sidney Poitier becomes the first black man to win an Academy Award, for *Lilies of the Field*.

1969: Gordon Parks becomes the first black man to direct a major Hollywood film: *The Learning Tree*.

1977: Lina Wertmüller becomes the first woman to be nominated for an Academy Award for Best Director.

1985: Prince becomes the first black man to win an Academy Award for Best Original Song Score, for *Purple Rain*.

1986: *The Oprah Winfrey Show* airs its first national episode. Oprah becomes the first black woman to host a daytime television talk show.

1992: John Singleton becomes the first black man to be nominated for an Academy Award for Best Director.

1997: Ellen DeGeneres publicly states that she is a lesbian and her character on her show also comes out.

1998: *Smoke Signals*, a movie based on a short story by Native American author Sherman Alexie, is released, featuring an all-Native American cast and crew.

1998: Fernanda Montenegro becomes the first Latinx to be nominated for an Academy Award for Best Actress.

1999: Hilary Swank wins an Academy Award for her portrayal of the real-life Brandon Teena, a transgender man, in the movie *Boys Don't Cry*.

2001: Denzel Washington becomes the first black man to win two Academy Awards for acting.

2001: Halle Berry becomes the first black woman to win an Academy Award for Best Actress, for *Monster's Ball*.

2005: Ang Lee becomes the first person of color to win the Academy Award for Best Director, for *Brokeback Mountain*.

2009: Princess Tiana in Disney's *The Princess and the Frog* becomes the first black Disney princess.

2010: Kathryn Bigelow becomes the first woman to win the Academy Award for Best Director, for *The Hurt Locker*.

2013: Alfonso Cuarón becomes the first Latinx to win an Academy Award for Best Director.

2014: Transgender actress Laverne Cox is nominated for an Emmy for her portrayal of a transgender inmate in Netflix's *Orange Is the New Black*.

2015: Viola Davis becomes the first black woman to win an Emmy for Outstanding Lead Actress in a Drama Series, for *How to Get Away with Murder*.

2018: *Crazy Rich Asians* is the first contemporary film in 25 years to be released by a major Hollywood studio and feature a majority Asian-American cast.

Glossary

advocates People who publicly support a cause or policy.

asynchronous development Development that is mismatched in the cognitive, emotional, and physical areas.

Augmentative and Alternative Communication (AAC) Communication methods used by individuals who are unable to speak or write in the traditional ways.

autism A developmental disorder characterized by different, often repetitive, patterns of thought and behavior, and sometimes difficulty in communication and/or social interaction.

civil rights movement A movement for social justice that took place from roughly 1954 to 1968, and involved black people working to gain equal rights to the white people of the United States.

dwarfism A medical condition resulting in small stature or size.

genre A category of musical composition in which songs share similarities in style, form, or subject.

Gold Rush The California Gold Rush of 1848 to 1855, in which hundreds of thousands of people came to California to search for gold.

Jim Crow laws State laws in the post–Civil War era that segregated black people from white people.

LGBTQ+ Acronym used to describe members of the lesbian, gay, bisexual, transgender, and queer/questioning community.

martial artists People who practice any of the martial arts, such as karate, judo, or taekwondo.

neurodiversity A range of differences in brain function and behavioral traits, considered part of the normal variation in humans.

norms Standard or patterns of behavior that are typical of a particular group.

one-dimensional Lacking depth; superficial.

ratified Made a treaty, contract, or agreement officially valid.

socioeconomic Related to the interaction of social and economic factors.

stereotypes Widely held but overly simple ideas about a particular type of person or thing.

Treacher Collins syndrome A genetic disorder that results in facial deformities involving the ears, eyes, cheekbones, and chin.

UNESCO Acronym for the United Nations Educational, Scientific and Cultural Organization, a part of the United Nations.

For Further Reading

Books

Alexie, Sherman. *The Absolutely True Diary of a Part-Time Indian*. New York, NY: Little, Brown, 2009.

Lace, William. *Blacks in Film*. Farmington Hills, MI: Lucent Library of Black History, 2008.

Malone, Alicia. *Backward and in Heels: The Past, Present and Future of Women Working in Film*. Miami, FL: Mango, 2018.

Wagman-Geller, Marlene. *Still I Rise: The Persistence of Phenomenal Women*. Miami, FL: Mango, 2017.

Websites

AMC Filmsite
www.filmsite.org/filmh.html/1910-filmhistory.html
This site aprovides timelines for important history and events in the film industry.

American Roots Music
www.pbs.org/americanrootsmusic
PBS offers this useful site covering the roots of American music.

Archive of American Television
www.emmytvlegends.org/resources/history
This site provides extensive history on television programming in the United States.

United States Census Bureau
www.census.gov/quickfacts/fact/table/US/PST045216
The Quick Facts page of the United States Census Bureau website is a great place to find data about the diverse groups of people that make up the United States.

Index

Academy Awards (Oscars) 6, 8, 14–15, 23, 25, 31, 32–33

disabilities
  autism 36, 38–39, 43
  cerebral palsy 34, 35, 40
  Down syndrome 35, 42
  dwarfism 42
  hiring actors with 39, 40
  intellectual 36, 37
    Radley, Boo 37
  Keller, Helen 37
  physical 35, 37
  representation 37, 38–39, 41
diversity
  abilities 5, 34–43
  cultural 28–33
  economic and social 22–27
  importance of 5, 7, 18–19, 25, 29, 31, 42–43
  racial 6–7, 10–15

Emmy Awards 9, 20, 21, 42
ethnic background
  Asian 4, 11, 12, 13, 15, 16, 17, 29
  black 4, 6, 10–12, 13, 14–15, 16, 17, 25, 28, 29, 31, 32–33
  Latinx 4, 6, 11, 13, 15, 16, 17, 29, 30, 32–33
  Middle Eastern 29, 43
  Native American 4, 11, 12, 13, 28–29, 30, 31
  white 4, 11, 12, 13, 15, 28, 31

film actors and actresses 4, 5, 8–9, 12, 14–15, 16, 23, 30, 32–33, 34, 35, 43
  Affleck, Ben 38
  Connelly, Jennifer 30
  Depp, Johnny 30
  Evans, Dale 35
  Fonda, Jane 8–9
  Foster, Jodie 23
  Goldberg, Whoopi 33
  Lawrence, Jennifer 16
  Lewis, Daniel Day- 34, 35
  McDaniel, Hattie 6
  McQueen, Steve 31

Nanjiani, Kumail 43
Nyong'o, Lupita 23, 32–33, 43
Poitier, Sidney 6, 14–15
Roberts, Julia 16
Stone, Emma 16
Streep, Meryl 16, 23
Swinton, Tilda 12
Tomlin, Lily 9
Watson, Emma 43
Zeta-Jones, Catherine 12
film industry 8
films 6, 12, 14, 21, 25, 30, 31, 33, 37, 38
  12 Years a Slave 31, 33
  A Beautiful Mind 30
  The Accountant 38
  The Color Purple 25
  Doctor Strange 12
  Finding Nemo 21
  Gone with the Wind 6
  Lilies of the Field 6, 14
  The Lone Ranger 30
  My Left Foot 34, 35
  No Way Out 14
  Smoke Signals 30
  Their Eyes Were Watching God 25
  To Kill a Mockingbird 37

Grammy Awards 7, 18, 26

Hollywood 4, 9, 14, 15, 16, 20

LGBTQ+ 16, 17, 19, 20–21

music industry 6–7, 18–19, 31
  diversity in 6–7, 18–19, 31
  racial inequality, history of 10–12
  role models 5, 18, 43
musicians 4, 6, 7, 13, 18, 23, 25, 26–27, 31, 35, 43
  Beyoncé 7, 43
  Bieber, Justin 25, 26–27
  Charles, Ray 6
  Durbin, James 43
  Fitzgerald, Ella 6
  Gomez, Selena 7
  Pink 43
  Presley, Elvis 6
  Prince 44

Swift, Taylor 7, 18
Wray, Link 31

stereotypes 5, 9, 13, 18, 29, 42, 43

television actors, actresses, and personalities 5, 20–21, 24–25, 33, 38, 39, 40–41, 42
  DeGeneres, Ellen 20–21
  Fowler, Micah 5, 40–41
  Gilchrist, Keir 39
  Highmore, Freddie 38
  Potter, Lauren 42
  Tremblay, Jacob 39
  Winfrey, Oprah 21, 24–25, 33
television industry and executives 8, 40
television shows 5, 9, 20, 21, 24–25, 29, 38, 39, 40–41, 42, 43
  American Idol 43
  Atypical 39
  Born This Way 42
  Ellen 20, 21
  The Ellen DeGeneres Show 21
  Glee 21, 42
  The Good Doctor 38
  Grace and Frankie 9
  Homeland 29
  Modern Family 21
  The Oprah Winfrey Show 20, 21, 24–25
  Speechless 5, 40–41
  The Tonight Show 20
  Will and Grace 21
  Wonder 39
Tony Awards 9

whitewashing 12, 14, 30
women 5, 6, 7, 8–9, 16–19